Living Things and Their Habitats

Welcome to the Rainforest

by Honor Head

Ruby Tuesday Books

Published in 2017 by Ruby Tuesday Books Ltd.

Editor: Jean Coppendale
Designer: Emma Randall
Consultant: Sally Morgan
Production: John Lingham

Photo credits
Alamy: 28 (left); FLPA: 6 (main), 7 (main), 8, 12, 17 (top left), 19, 20 (right), 23 (bottom), 25 (bottom); Shutterstock: Cover, 2–3, 4–5, 6 (left), 7 (top), 9, 10–11, 13, 14–15, 16, 17 (top right), 17 (bottom), 18, 20 (left), 21, 22, 23 (top), 24, 25 (top), 26–27, 28 (right), 30–31; Superstock: 29.

British Library Cataloguing in Publication Data (CIP) is available for this title.

ISBN 978-1-911341-54-3

Printed in Poland by L&C Printing Group

www.rubytuesdaybooks.com

Contents

Words shown in **bold** in the text are explained in the glossary.

Welcome to the Rainforest

Who and what lives in the wet, hot, steamy Amazon rainforest?

This **habitat** is home to tall trees, ferns and many other plants.

The animals that live in this habitat include jaguars, birds and frogs.

Every living thing in the rainforest gets what it needs to live from its habitat.

A rainforest is one of the wettest places on Earth. It is made up of four layers, the forest floor, the understorey, the canopy and the top, or emergent trees. Very little sunlight reaches the ground through the thick trees.

Let's explore the Amazon rainforest floor!

On the Rainforest Floor

The rainforest floor is dark and damp.

It is covered with a layer of **leaf litter**.

This is made up of fallen trees, branches, leaves, flowers and fruit.

Cup fungi

Fungi feed on the rotting plants.

In the steamy forest, the leaf litter soon rots and becomes part of the soil. The trees take up the **nutrients** they need to be healthy from the soil.

Millipedes help recycle dead leaves by eating them.

Their poo, which is filled with nutrients, gets mixed into the soil.

Millipede

Agouti

An agouti finds a feast of fallen fruit.

What happens to some of the rain that falls on the forest?

7

A Very Wet Habitat

The rain that falls on the forest creates rivers, lakes and swampy areas.

Armadillos live on the forest floor near water.

Armadillo

To help them swim, armadillos gulp in air to inflate, or blow up, their intestines. This makes them lighter in the water so they don't sink.

They use the rivers to move from place to place, and to escape from **predators** that want to eat them.

Armadillos use their snouts to dig for beetles in the leaf litter.

They also feed on ants and termites.

They have a long, sticky tongue that can slurp up lots of insects in one go.

A termite mound, or nest

An armadillo digging for food

Termite

Which forest animal lives on land but has webbed feet?

9

Meet the Capybaras

Some rainforest animals live on land and in water.

Capybaras live on land but are also excellent swimmers and divers.

Capybara

They use the water to keep cool when it is hot.

Capybaras jump into rivers and lakes to escape from predators, such as snakes and jaguars.

A capybara has webbed feet for swimming. When it dives underwater, it can press its ears against its head to keep the water out.

An adult capybara is the size of a large pig.

Webbed feet

What danger is lurking in the trees that hang over the river?

HISSS!

Above the forest floor is a tangle of bushes and small trees called the understorey.

Huge, brown snakes called anacondas live in the understorey.

Anaconda

A female anaconda can grow to be more than 5 metres long.

An anaconda hunts on the ground for capybaras.

Its colour and patterns make it difficult to see among the plants.

It also slides into the water to catch birds, turtles and caimans.

Turtle

Caiman

Caimans have strong jaws and sharp teeth to fight off anacondas and other predators.

What other hunter wants to have a caiman for dinner?

A Big Cat in the Forest

The jaguar is a top predator in the Amazon rainforest.

It eats capybaras, caimans and other forest animals – but nothing eats the jaguar!

Jaguar

A jaguar's spotted coat helps it to blend in with the sunlight coming through the trees. Its padded paws help it to move silently through the forest. It is difficult for **prey** to see or hear the jaguar coming.

A jaguar spots a caiman in a river and slips into the water.

She grabs the caiman by the back of its neck.

One strong bite, and the caiman is dead!

Then the jaguar pulls the heavy caiman up the riverbank so she can feed.

Caiman

What will we find if we climb higher up into the trees?

The Rainforest Canopy

Above the understorey is the green and leafy canopy.

This layer of the forest is made up of the top parts of the trees.

The branches and leaves form a thick, roof-like covering over the forest.

The canopy

A three-toed sloth eating leaves

Nearly all the animals that live in the Amazon rainforest live in the canopy. The trees and other plants provide leaves, flowers, nuts and berries for them to eat.

Ferns growing on a branch

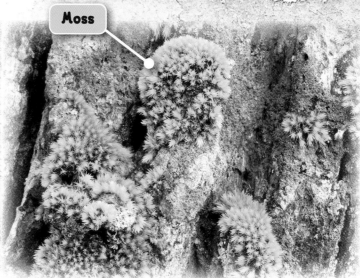

Moss

Bromeliad

The trees are home to ferns, bromeliads and tiny moss plants.

One tree can have thousands of other plants growing on its trunk and branches.

What animal is making a loud howling noise in the canopy?

Life in the Canopy

Howler monkey

The air is filled with howls, shrieks and screams.

These noises are monkeys communicating with each other.

Squirrel monkey

The howl of a howler monkey can be heard for many kilometres across the forest.

Monkeys sleep, find food and travel around the forest in the trees.

Prehensile tail

Spider monkey

Most monkeys never touch the forest floor.

They swing from tree to tree or run along branches.

Some monkeys have a long, **prehensile** tail that they use like another arm.

The tail can be curled around a branch to help them balance or leave their hands free for grabbing food.

What other noisy animals are looking for food in the trees?

Birds and Beaks

The birds that live in the canopy have a feast of insects, fruit and nuts to feed on.

They have different-shaped beaks to help them eat their favourite foods.

Jacamar

Toucan

A jacamar catches a butterfly in its slim, pointed beak.

A toucan uses its long beak to reach for fruit.

A macaw's sharp, hooked beak can split open nuts and fruit.

Macaw

A sword-billed hummingbird's beak is longer than its body. Its extra-long beak can reach the **nectar** deep inside flowers.

Sword-billed hummingbird

When is a leaf not a leaf?

21

When is a Leaf Not a Leaf?

When it is an insect! Some small creatures have developed a way to trick birds and other animals that might want to eat them.

These animals look like a dead leaf or tree trunk that is not very tasty.

A katydid insect

Dead leaves on the forest floor

Katydid insects look like the leaves of the trees they feed on.

This is called mimicry.

Katydid

This little tree frog looks like a part of the tree trunk.

This is called camouflage.

People say katydids make a noise that sounds like someone saying, "Katy did, Katy did". This is how they got their name.

What tiny animal uses a bromeliad plant as a swimming pool?

Fit for a Frog!

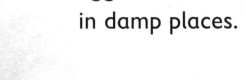

Bromeliad pool

Some bromeliads have stiff, upright leaves that act like a bowl to collect rainwater.

These little pools of water are very helpful to tiny poison dart frogs.

A red-backed poison dart frog

The frogs lay their eggs on leaves or in damp places.

When tadpoles hatch, the parent frogs carry them up into the towering trees.

Tadpoles

A sky-blue poison dart frog

There are lots of rivers and ponds in a rainforest, but these watery places are home to fish and other predators. A bromeliad pool, high up a tree, is a safe place for a tadpole to live.

They place each tadpole in its own bromeliad.

Inside its tiny pool, the tadpole grows and changes into a frog.

Tadpole

How high do the tallest rainforest trees grow?

Top Trees

The tallest trees in the rainforest grow above the canopy to form the top, or emergent, layer.

Kapok tree

Bat

Giant kapok trees grow to over 60 metres tall!

Birds, monkeys and bats live in these trees.

Kapok trees grow flowers that produce seeds in large pods.

Seedpod

Kapok tree flower

Kapok tree flower

The tiny seeds are in white floss that is blown about by the wind.

The seeds float to the ground so new trees can grow.

Bats visit the flowers to feast on nectar. As they feed, the bats become covered in **pollen**. They carry the pollen from tree to tree. This helps the flowers make seeds.

Floss

Seedpod

Seed

Which powerful predator is hunting for monkeys in the treetops?

A Treetop Predator

Harpy eagle

The eagle's wings are nearly 2 metres wide.

A harpy eagle is hunting in the treetops.

She uses her super sharp **talons** and strong legs to snatch a howler monkey from a branch.

Howler monkey

Then she carries the monkey back to her nest to feed to her chick.

A pair of harpy eagles build their nest in a kapok tree.

When an eagle finds a branch it wants for its nest, it grabs it with its talons. Then the eagle flaps its wings until the branch breaks off.

Harpy eagle chick

The nest is big enough to fit two people inside!

An old nest falls down to the forest floor.

Soon the nest rots and becomes part of the leaf litter that feeds the rainforest trees.

A Rainforest Food Web

A food web shows who eats who in a habitat.

This food web shows the connections between some of the living things in a rainforest.

Plants make the food they need for energy and growth in their leaves. To do this they need sunlight.

The arrows mean: **eaten by**

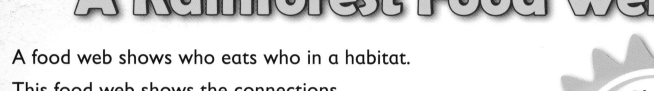

Jaguar

Caiman

Harpy eagle

Anaconda

Insects

Armadillo

Toucan

Capybara

Plants

Monkey

Glossary

fungi
A group of living things that
includes mushrooms.

habitat
The place where an
animal or plant lives.
Rainforests, deserts
and gardens are all
types of habitats.

intestines
Long tubes where an animal's or person's
food is digested, or broken down, after
it leaves the stomach.

leaf litter
Leaves, twigs, flowers
and fruit that fall to the
ground from trees and
other plants.

nectar
A sugary
liquid produced
by flowers.

nutrients
Substances that living things
need to grow, get energy and
be healthy.

pollen
A coloured dust that is made
by flowers, and is needed for
making seeds.

predator
An animal that hunts and
eats other animals.

prehensile
Able to grasp or hold on to something.

prey
An animal that is hunted
by other animals for food.

talons
Long, sharp claws on
the feet of a hunting
bird such as an eagle or owl.

Index

A
anacondas 12–13, 30
armadillos 8–9, 30

B
bats 26–27
birds 4–5, 13, 20–21, 22, 26, 28–29, 30
bromeliads 17, 23, 24–25

C
caimans 13, 14–15, 30
canopy 5, 16–17, 18–19, 20, 26
capybaras 10–11, 13, 14, 30

E
emergent layer 5, 26–27

F
ferns 4, 17
flowers 6, 16, 21, 27
forest floor 5, 6–7, 8, 12, 19, 22, 29
frogs 4, 23, 24–25
fruit 6–7, 20–21

H
harpy eagles 28–29, 30

I
insects 9, 20, 22–23, 30

J
jaguars 4, 11, 14–15, 30

K
kapok trees 26–27, 29

L
leaf litter 6–7, 9, 29

M
millipedes 7
monkeys 18–19, 26–27, 28, 30

N
nuts 16, 20–21

P
predators 8–9, 11, 13, 14–15, 20, 22, 25, 27, 28, 30
prey 8–9, 11, 13, 14–15, 20, 22, 25, 28, 30

T
tadpoles 25
turtles 13

U
understorey 5, 12, 16

Learn More Online

To learn more about life in a rainforest, go to
www.rubytuesdaybooks.com/habitats